LOOK 2

WORKBOOK

Rachel Wilson

COURSE CONSULTANTS

Elaine Boyd

Paul Dummett

NATIONAL GEOGRAPHIC
LEARNING

Australia • Brazil • Mexico • Singapore • United Kingdom • United States

NATIONAL GEOGRAPHIC
L E A R N I N G

National Geographic Learning,
a Cengage Company

Look 2 Workbook

Author: Rachel Wilson

Course Consultants: Elaine Boyd and Paul Dummett

Publisher: Sherrise Roehr

Publishing Consultant: Karen Spiller

Executive Editor: Eugenia Corbo

Project Manager: Laura Brant

Director of Global Marketing: Ian Martin

Heads of Regional Marketing:

  Charlotte Ellis (Europe, Middle East and Africa)

  Kiel Hamm (Asia)

  Irina Pereyra (Latin America)

Product Marketing Manager: Dave Spain

Senior Director, Production: Michael Burggren

Senior Content Project Manager: Nick Ventullo

Media Researcher: Leila Hishmeh

Art Director: Brenda Carmichael

Manufacturing Buyer: Elaine Bevan

Composition: Composure Graphics, LLC

For permission to use material from this text or product, submit all requests online at **cengage.com/permissions**
Further permissions questions can be emailed to **permissionrequest@cengage.com**

Workbook ISBN: 978-1-337-90858-0
Workbook + Online Practice ISBN: 978-0-357-12204-4

National Geographic Learning
Cheriton House, North Way,
Andover, Hampshire, SP10 5BE
United Kingdom

Locate your local office at **international.cengage.com/region**

Visit National Geographic Learning online at **ELTNGL.com**
Visit our corporate website at **www.cengage.com**

Printed in the United Kingdom by Ashford Colour Press Ltd.
Print Number: 06   Print Year: 2023

Contents

Look 2 WORKBOOK

1 **Listen and colour.** 🎧 TR: 1

2 **Make suggestions.**

> fly a kite   ~~go to the swimming pool~~   make a cake
> paint a picture   read a book

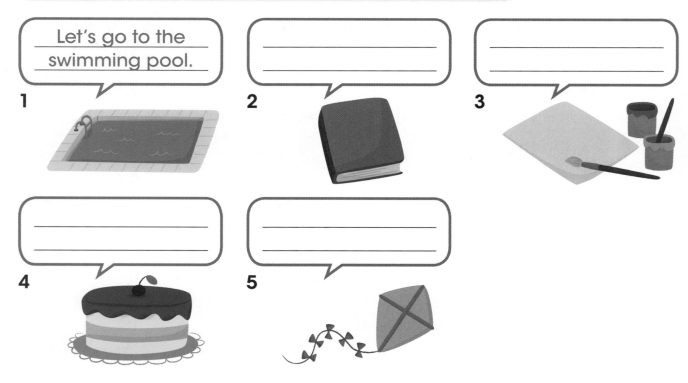

1 Let's go to the swimming pool.

2

3

4

5

3 **Write about the picture.**

1 How many scarecrows are there? There's <u>1/one scarecrow</u>.

2 There _____ cows.

3 There are _____ dogs.

4 How many chickens _____? There _____.

5 _____ many ducks are there? There _____.

6 _____ flowers.

4 **Write.**

1 (walk / run)
The baby
_____<u>can walk</u>_____.
_____<u>She can't run</u>_____.

2 (run / fly) My brother
_____.
_____.

3 (talk) Can a donkey talk?
_____.

4 (sing) _____?
Yes, it can.

1 Label the parts of the body.

1 _____

2 _____

3 _____

4 _____

5 _____

6 This girl can play _____.

2 Read and write.

aunt   brother   ~~cupboard~~   grandpa   library   playground
shower   sofa   shop   swimming pool   table   uncle

Home	Town	Family
cupboard		

3 **Read and circle.**

1 I **have got** / **has got** a lamp in my bedroom.

2 My cousin **have got** / **has got** a clock in her kitchen.

3 I **haven't got** / **hasn't got** a sofa in my bedroom.

4 My brother **haven't got** / **hasn't got** a TV in his bedroom.

5 **Have** / **Has** you got a TV in your living room?

6 **Have** / **Has** your aunt got a shower in her bathroom?

4 **Listen and draw ☺ or ☹.** 🎧 TR: 2

1

2

3

4

5

6

5 **Write two foods you like and two foods you don't like.**

1 ☺ _____

2 ☹ _____

Back to school

Words

1 Match.

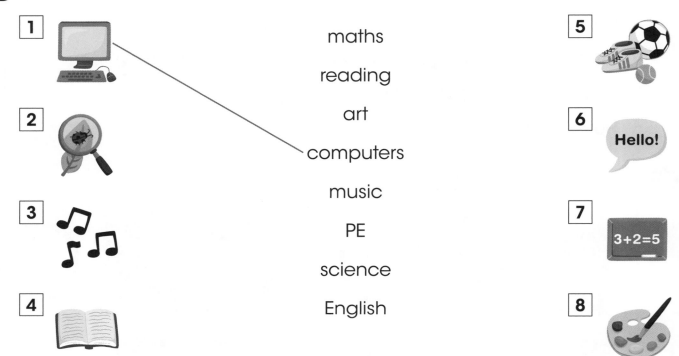

1

2

3

4

maths

reading

art

computers

music

PE

science

English

5

6

Hello!

7

3+2=5

8

2 Listen and circle. 🎧 TR: 3

1 music	(Yes) / No	science	Yes / No
2 art	Yes / No	maths	Yes / No
3 PE	Yes / No	reading	Yes / No
4 English	Yes / No	computers	Yes / No

3 What do you like? Write in order (☹ to ☺).

1 **Listen and write.** 🎧 TR: 4

Monday, Tuesday – time for school!
Wednesday, Thursday, Friday – time for school!

I've got English on _____ , time for school.
I've got maths _____ Tuesday, time for school.
I've got art _____ , time for school.
_____ music on Thursday, time for school.
_____ . School is cool!

Saturday, Sunday, there's no school.
There's no school. That's cool too!

2 **Read and tick (✓). Which student has got this timetable?**

Monday	Tuesday	Wednesday	Thursday	Friday
reading	PE	English	maths	English
science	maths	reading	science	PE
LUNCH				
maths	English	music	English	reading
art	science	maths	computers	maths

1 ☐ I've got reading on Monday and Thursday.

2 ☐ I've got PE on Tuesday and computers on Wednesday.

3 ☐ I've got art on Monday and music on Wednesday.

3 **Write about your week.**

1 I've got PE _____ .

2 I've got art _____ .

3 I've got music _____ .

4 I've got English _____ .

1 Unscramble the words.

1 dengar _g a r d e n_

2 solsne _ _ _ _ _ _

3 korwmohe _ _ _ _ _ _ _ _

4 sclas _ _ _ _ _

2 Read and write. 🎧 TR: 5

| classes   farm   garden   homework   lesson   students |

Welcome to the Green School in Bali, Indonesia. It's a very cool school. At the Green School, _____ learn about animals and plants. A classroom at the Green School hasn't got normal walls or windows. The classrooms are open, and students can see the plants and trees.

From Monday to Friday, there are _____ in English, maths, computers, music, art, reading and PE. There's _____ too. At the Green School, every _____ has got a _____. There are garden lessons on Wednesday and Thursday. There are flowers, rice and fruit in the garden. There's a _____ too. Students give food and water to the animals on the farm.

3 Read and tick (✓) or cross (✗).

	Green School	My school
1 There's a garden at the school.	✓	☐
2 There's a farm at the school.	☐	☐
3 The classrooms have got walls and windows.	☐	☐
4 There's homework at the school.	☐	☐

4 Write about your school.

There's a _____ at my school. There's also a _____ . The classrooms have got _____ .

1 Circle.

1 Have (you) / **she** / **he** got English on Monday?

Yes, **I** / **she** / **he** have.

2 Has **I** / **you** / **he** got PE on Thursday?

No, **I** / **you** / **he** hasn't.

2 Listen and write *Sofia* or *Marissa*. 🎧 TR: 6

1 _____   **2** _____

3 Look and write.

1 Has Marissa got her homework book?   _____

2 Has Sofia got her PE shoes?   _____

3 Has Marissa got a banana?   _____

4 Has Marissa got a pencil case?   _____

5 Has Sofia got an apple?   _____

6 Has Sofia got her school hat?   _____

1 **Listen and number.** 🎧 TR: 7

tank ☐   maths ☐   bat ☐

thank 1   mat ☐   bath ☐

2 **Help the monkey find the bananas. Circle the words with *th*. Say.**

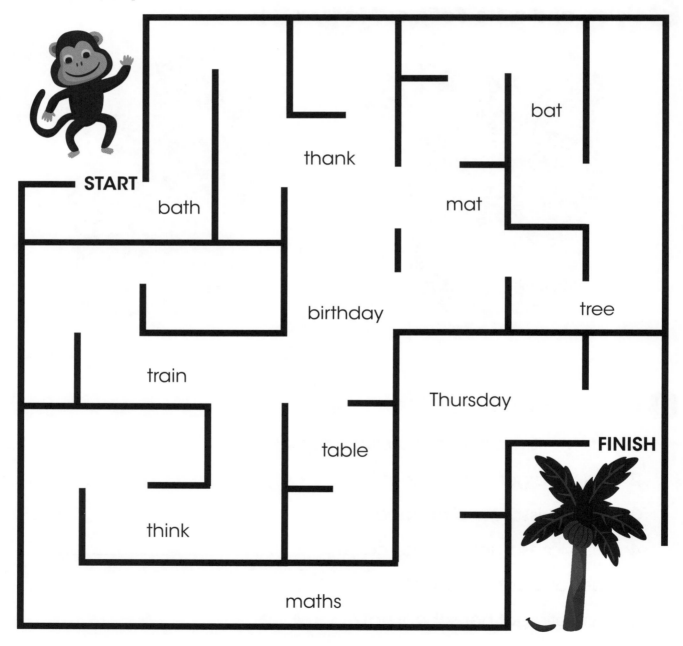

1 **Who is being responsible? Look and tick (✓).**

1

2

2 **Read. Put the actions in order.**

After school …

1 I play with my toys. `2`

   I do my science homework. `1`

2 I give my cat her dinner. ☐

   I play football. ☐

3 I watch TV. ☐

   I help my mum in the house. ☐

3 **Draw a picture of you being responsible at school or at home.**

1 Listen and number. Colour. 🎧 TR: 8

☐   ☐ 1   ☐   ☐

2 Match and write.

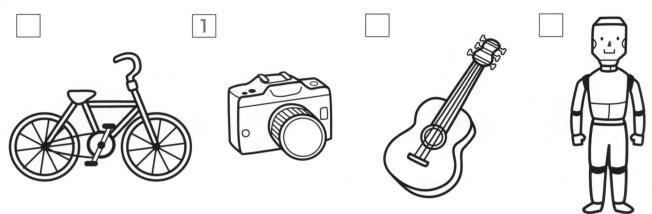

1 It's a _____robot_____ .

2 It's a _____ .

3 They're _____ .

4 It's a _____ .

5 It's a _____ .

6 They're _____ .

7 It's a _____ .

8 It's a _____ .

3 Which of these things have you got? Write.

I've got _____ .

1 Listen and write. 🎧 TR: 9

Is _____ your skateboard? Can I have a go?

Yes, _____ my skateboard. You can have a go!

Are _____ your building bricks? Can I have a go?

Yes, _____ my building bricks. You can have a go!

2 Look, read and tick (✓).

1

This is my skateboard. ✓

That's my skateboard. ☐

2

This isn't my bike. ☐

That isn't my bike. ☐

3

These are my felt-tip pens. ☐

Those are my felt-tip pens. ☐

4

These aren't my pencils. ☐

Those aren't my pencils. ☐

3 Draw and write.

This is my _____ .

These are my _____ .

1 **Circle the words that are opposites.**

borrow cool new old

2 **Listen and write.** 🎧 TR: 10 | borrow cool new old robots short

Claudia Chan Shaw is a toy collector in Australia. She's got lots of _____ toys. Claudia has got old and _____ toys. She really likes toy _____ . Look at these robots from her collection!

Claudia has got a robot called Robby. Robby is black. His head is big. His arms and feet are red. He can walk!

Claudia has got another robot called Zoomer. He's more than sixty years old! He's got _____ arms and legs. Zoomer's body is blue. He can walk too.

You can't _____ or play with Claudia's toys. They're too _____ . But you can watch videos of them on your computer.

3 **Look at Robby. Tick (✓) or cross (✗).**

1 He's got big feet. ✓   **4** He's got short arms. ☐

2 He's got a small head. ✗   **5** He can walk. ☐

3 He's got short legs. ☐   **6** He can run. ☐

4 **Draw a robot. Write about it.**

1 My robot is called _____ .

2 It's got _____ .

3 It can _____ .

1 Read and circle.

1 This is **Sams** / **Sam's** bike.

2 These aren't **Tilly's** / **Tilly** marbles.

3 That's **Zane's** / **Zanes** camera.

4 Those are **Jodys** / **Jody's** building bricks.

2 Listen, look and write. Does it belong to Jakob or Zara? 🎧 TR: 11

1  This is _Jakob's_ guitar.

2  This is _____ guitar.

3  This is _____ camera.

4  This is _____ camera.

3 Look and write.

Yui

Sana

1 It is _____Yui's_____ ball.

2 It is _____ skateboard.

3 It _____ bike.

4 It _____ bag.

5 It _____ hat.

1 **Listen and circle the words with *th* as in *this*.** 🎧 TR: 12

(this)   bath   that   these   maths   those

thank   brother   Thursday   mother   three   think

2 **Colour *red* the parts with *th* like in *this*. Say. What's the secret picture?**

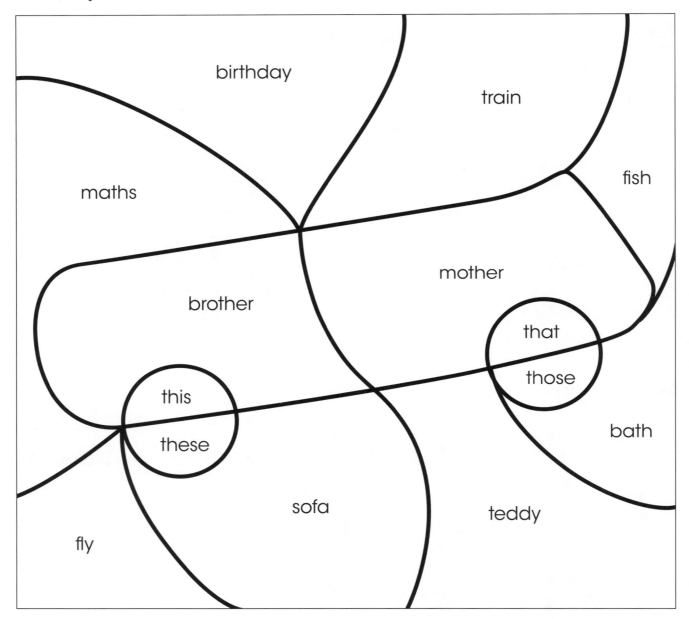

birthday

train

fish

maths

mother

brother

that

those

this

these

bath

fly

sofa

teddy

The secret picture is _____ .

1 Who is being tidy? Read and tick (✓).

2 Draw lines to tidy up the bedroom.

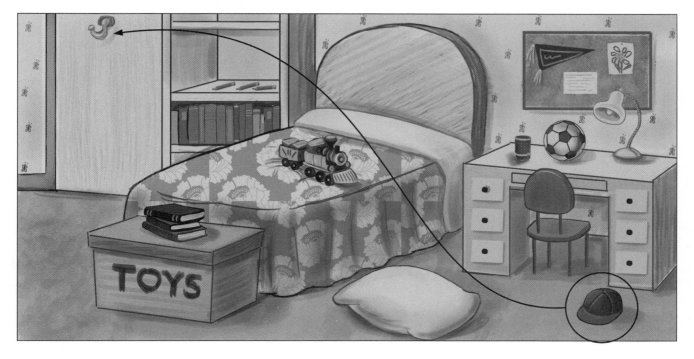

1 **Read and circle. Listen and check.** 🎧 TR: 13

Enrico: Hi, Lee. How are (you) / **they** feeling today?

Lee: I haven't got a drink, so I'm feeling **thirsty / hungry**.

Enrico: Oh, no! Here, have some water.

Lee: Thanks. And you? **How are / Where are** you feeling?

Enrico: Not good. I'm feeling **angry / tired**.

Lee: Oh, no! What's **the matter / the homework**?

Enrico: I can't find my pencil.

Lee: Here. You can borrow my pencil.

Enrico: Great, thanks. Now I'm feeling **sad / happy**!

2 **Look and write.**

1
How are you feeling today?
I'm feeling ___tired___ .

2
What's the matter?
I'm _____ .

3
Are you OK?
I'm _____ , thanks.

4
How _____ feeling today?
I'm feeling sad.

5
What's _____ ?
Nothing's the matter!

6
Are _____ ?
I'm fine, thanks.

1 Remember the video. Circle the robots that you saw.

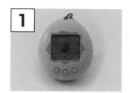 1  2  3  4

2 Read and write.

ASIMO the robot

It's the school _____science_____
trip to the Miraikan museum.
Today, the students can see a real
_____ called ASIMO.
ASIMO is a 'humanoid' robot –
it looks a bit like a _____.
It's got a head, but it hasn't
got eyes. ASIMO's 'eyes' are a

_____. It's got a body, two arms and two legs. It can walk
and run. It can even _____! But it can't feel happy or
_____ like you or me. It hasn't got feelings.

~~science~~

man

sad

robot

jump

camera

1 Find, circle and write.

r	m	u	c	o	o	l	s
s	m	a	t	h	s	p	h
w	h	i	k	d	n	e	w
h	o	m	e	w	o	r	k
e	g	a	r	d	e	n	n
r	e	a	d	i	n	g	y

1 c <u>o</u> <u>o</u> <u>l</u>

2 m _ _ _ _ _

3 n _ _

4 h _ _ _ _ _ _ _

5 g _ _ _ _ _

6 r _ _ _ _ _ _

2 Circle the odd one out.

1

building bricks   camera   tablet

2

PE lesson   art lesson   robot

3

bike   guitar   skateboard

4

felt-tip pens   music lesson   tablet

3 Read and write the words in the correct column of the table.

~~bath~~ birthday brother thank that those

Words with *th* like in *maths*	Words with *th* like in *this*
bath	

4 Look, read and circle.

1  (This is a garden.) / These are gardens.

2 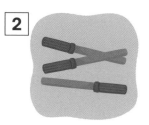 This is a felt-tip pen. / These are felt-tip pens.

3 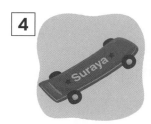 I've got music on Tuesday. / I've got music on Thursday.

4  This is Amita's skateboard. / This isn't Amita's skateboard.

5 Read and write.

1 Have you got science on Monday?   Yes, _____I have_____.

2 Are those your felt-tip pens?   No, _____.

3 Has she got science on Monday?   No, _____.

4 Has he got science on Monday?   Yes, _____.

5 Is this Milo's homework?   No, _____.

I can ...	Yes.	I need to practise.
• name school subjects and my things.	☐	☐
• talk about school days.	☐	☐
• ask and answer questions with *Have you got ... ?* and *Has he/she got ... ?*	☐	☐
	☐	☐
• use *this, that, these* and *those* to talk about people's things.	☐	☐
• use apostrophes: *Kevin's guitar.*	☐	☐
• read and spell words with *th.*	☐	☐

LESSON 1 Words

1 **Listen and circle.** 🎧 TR: 14

dining room   mirror   bookcase   rug   floor

balcony   window   ⟨armchair⟩   door

2 **Label the dining room.**

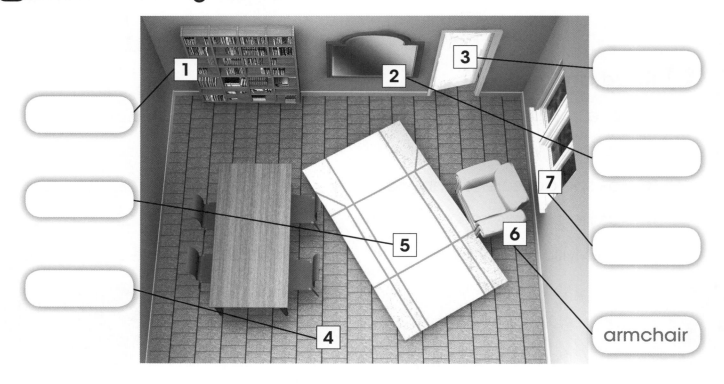

armchair

3 **Colour the door, rug and armchair in Exercise 2.**
Write about them.

In my picture …

1 There's a _____ door.

2 There's a _____ .

3 There's a _____ .

1 Listen and write. 🎧 TR: 15

This is our home. This is _____ dining room.
That's their home. That's _____ dining room.

We've _____ a blue door and a rug on the floor.
They've _____ a blue door and a rug on the floor.

_____ a balcony with lots to see.
_____ a balcony with lots to see.

2 Read and circle.

This is Paolo and Maria. This is **their** / **your** tree house. They've **have** / **got** a rug on the floor. **We've** / **They've** got a bookcase with books and toys. They **'ve got** / **'s got** a guitar too. **Their** / **Our** tree house is cool!

3 Draw a tree house for you and your friend. Write about it.

This is _____
tree house.

We've got a _____
and an _____ .

We've _____ .

3 Reading

1 Circle the words that are opposites.

inside   stairs   wall   outside

2 Read and write. 🎧 TR: 16

climb   inside   outside   stairs   swing   wall

This is a plan for a small house in Denmark. Imagine we're in front of the door. Let's go _____!

There's a white armchair under the kitchen. Let's go up the _____. There's a swing. A bookcase is behind the swing. I can sit on the _____ and read. What fun!

There's a bedroom and a small room with a computer. The bathroom is between these rooms.

Look! There's a climbing _____. We haven't got that in our house. Let's _____! I can see a garden with flowers. There's a balcony _____ too. This house is super cool!

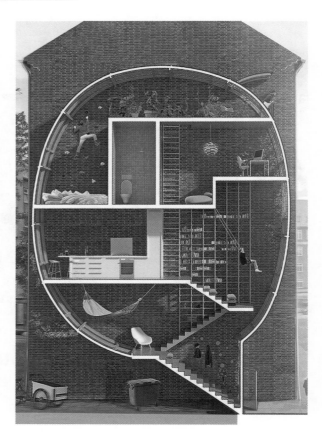

3 What are your favourite things about this house? Write.

My favourite things about this house are _____ and _____.

1 Read and match.

1 The book is in front of the lamp.

2 The book is between the apple and the pencils.

3 The book is behind the computer.

2 Listen and circle the things that you hear. 🎧 TR: 17

3 Look at the bedroom and write.

ball ~~bat~~ between bookcase door in front of

1 There's a ____bat____ _____ the desk and the bed.

2 There's a _____ behind the _____ .

3 There's a guitar _____ the _____ .

1 Listen and join the words. 🎧 TR: 18

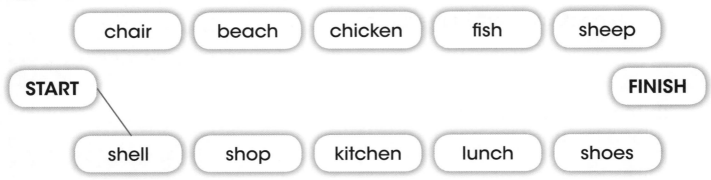

| chair | beach | chicken | fish | sheep |

START   **FINISH**

| shell | shop | kitchen | lunch | shoes |

2 Colour *yellow* the words with *ch*. Colour *blue* the words with *sh*. Say.

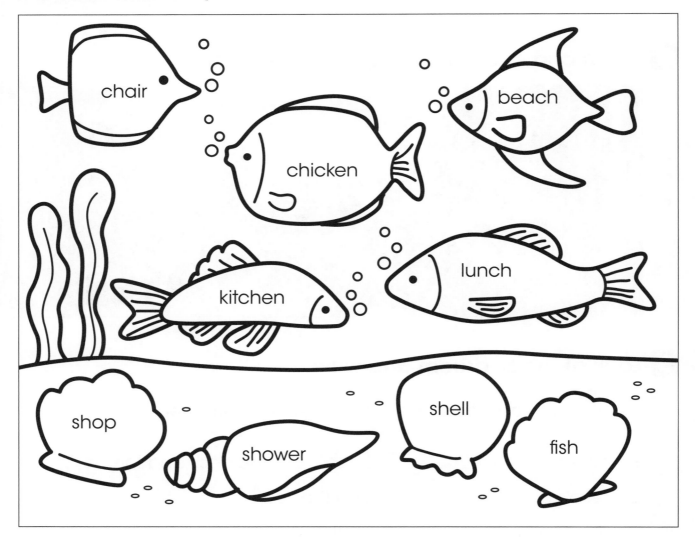

1 **Who is accepting differences? Look and tick (✓).**

☐ You've got a balcony. That's great!

☐ My house isn't the same as yours. You haven't got a garden. That isn't good.

☐ What's in your lunch box? It isn't the same as my lunch. It doesn't look good.

☐ I like your lunch. You've got rice and chicken. That looks good!

2 **Think of something that you've got that isn't the same as your friend's. Draw to show the differences.**

You

Your friend

LESSON 1 Words

1 Find the words. Circle.

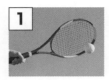
1

2

3

a	l	b	o	u	n	c	e
c	a	t	c	h	s	d	g
i	m	h	i	t	o	j	a
d	k	j	u	m	p	p	a
e	r	v	k	i	c	k	i
s	r	g	t	h	r	o	w

4

5

6

2 Listen and number. Write. 🎧 TR: 19

[ ]

[ ]

[ ]

1

3 What do you do in each sport? Write.

bounce x 2   catch x 2   hit x 3   jump x 4   kick x 1   throw x 4

football	hockey	basketball	tennis	baseball
jump kick throw				

1 **Listen and write.** 🎧 TR: 20

We _____ baseball in the park,
and it's fun, fun, fun!
_____ throw, hit and catch the ball.
Then _____, run, run!

_____ run, jump and catch the ball.
Then _____, throw, throw!
We _____ or bounce the ball
In baseball. No, no, no!

2 **Put the words in order. Match.**

1 I / friends / hockey / play /
with / my

_____ I play hockey with my friends. _____

A

B

2 kick / don't / the / you / ball /
in / baseball

_____

C

3 tennis / play / they / outside

_____

4 we / basketball / run / the / with /
ball / don't / in

D

_____

3 **What sport do you play with your friends? Draw and write.**

We play _____.

We _____.

We don't _____.

1 Circle the word that means *great*. Underline the word that is a *group of people*.

different   easy   fantastic   team

2 Read and write. 🎧 TR: 21

basket   different   easy   fantastic   team

Do you like basketball? Lots of people do. It's very popular. In basketball, you run and bounce the ball. You throw it to a player on your _____. You catch it, then you jump. You throw the ball in the _____, and … score!

Players in the King Charles Troupe bounce, throw and catch the ball, but their game is _____. They don't run – they play on unicycles! A unicycle is like a bike, but with one wheel, not two. It isn't _____, but the players in the King Charles Troupe can bounce, throw and catch a ball – all on their unicycles. They're _____! Lots of people watch them play.

Can you play basketball? Can you ride a unicycle? Maybe you can be in the King Charles Troupe too!

3 Answer the questions.

1 Is basketball popular?   _____

2 Do players on the team run with the ball?   _____

3 Has a unicycle got two wheels?   _____

4 Do you play a team sport?   _____

5 What sport is easy for you?   _____

1 Read and circle.

1 Do you play baseball inside?   No, we **do / don't**.

2 Do basketball players throw the ball into the basket?   Yes, they **do / don't**.

3 Do you hit the ball in tennis?   **Yes / No**, I do.

4 Do you ride your bikes outside?   Yes, we **do / don't**.

5 Do they score goals in football?   **Yes / No**, they do.

2 Listen and write. 🎧 TR: 22

1 _____ Yes, I do. _____

2 _____

3 _____

4 _____

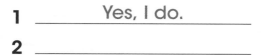

3 Write about you.

1

Do you play
_____?
_____.

2

Do you
_____?
_____.

3

Do
_____?
_____.

4

_____
_____?
_____.

1 **Listen and number.** 🎧 TR: 23

pink ☐   sock ☐   black ☐

thank ☐   duck ☐   sink ☐

2 **Help the climber to climb the rock. Write words with**
ck and nk. Say.

du   dri   ki   li   pi   ro   tha

duck

1 Who is keeping fit? Look and tick (✓).

It's Saturday.

Let's play games on our tablets.

1 ☐ OK. Good idea.

2 ☐ No, let's go outside and play.

After school.

Let's watch TV at home.

1 ☐ No, let's ride our bikes.

2 ☐ Yeah, OK.

2 What can you do to keep fit? Tick (✓).

play basketball ☐   watch TV ☐   fly your kite ☐

play on your tablet ☐   go for a walk ☐   play football ☐

3 Read and draw.

Look at me! I'm keeping fit.

Game 1

1 Do the crossword.

1 t h r o w

4

5

2

3

6

7

8

9

10

11

12

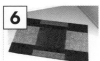

Let's go on an insect safari!

1 Listen. Tick (✓) what the students find on their insect safari. 🎧 TR: 24

beetle

bee

dragonfly

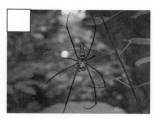
spider

2 Complete the table. Listen again to check your answers. 🎧 TR: 25

	lanternfly	blue dasher	golden orb-weaver
What is it?	a beetle		
How many legs has it got?			
What can it do?			

3 Imagine you're on an insect safari. What can you see? Draw and write.

This is a _____.

It's a _____.

It's got _____.

It can _____.

1 Unscramble the words.

1

o m r i r r
<u>m</u> <u>i</u> <u>r</u> <u>r</u> <u>o</u> <u>r</u>

2

o u n c e b
_ _ _ _ _ _

3

w o w d i n
_ _ _ _ _ _

4

m u p j
_ _ _ _

5

g r u
_ _ _

6

t h i
_ _ _

2 Match.

1 You walk up and down these.   fantastic

2 It's the opposite of *inside*.   rug

3 It's the opposite of *catch*.   dining room

4 It's on the floor.   stairs

5 You can have dinner here.   throw

6 It means *great*.   outside

3 Circle the odd one out: *ch, sh, ck, nk*.

1 chair   chicken   (sink)

2 think   ship   shower

3 sock   pink   sink

4 thank   think   fish

5 kitchen   shell   sheep

4 **Listen, draw and write.** 🎧 TR: 26

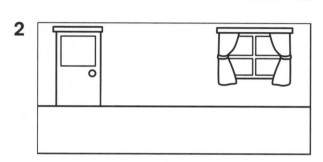

1

The tree is _____ the wall.
The basketball is _____
the tree.

2

The mirror is _____ the
door and the window. The rug is
_____ the floor.

5 **Read and answer.**

1 Do you play hockey at your school? _____

2 Have you got a balcony outside your house? _____

3 Have you got stairs inside your house? _____

4 Do you play basketball outside your house? _____

I can ...	Yes.	I need to practise.
• name things inside and outside my house.	☐	☐
• say words and actions for some sports.	☐	☐
• talk about what we/they have got in our/their house.	☐	☐
• ask and answer questions about where things are.	☐	☐
• ask and answer questions with *have got.*	☐	☐
• read and spell words with *ch*, *sh*, *ck* and *nk*.	☐	☐

1 Match.

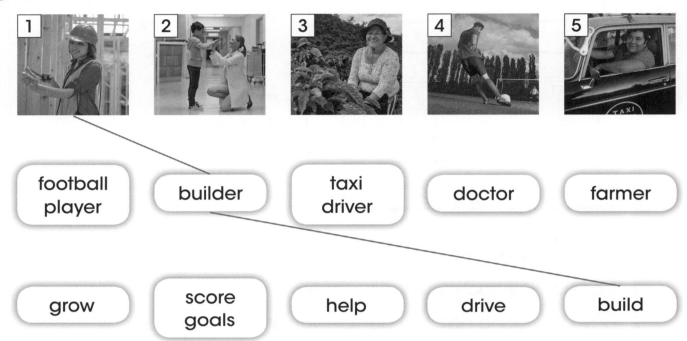

football player   builder   taxi driver   doctor   farmer

grow   score goals   help   drive   build

2 Listen and circle. 🎧 TR: 27

1 builder   doctor   2 teacher   doctor

3 taxi driver   farmer   4 football player   basketball player

3 Write.

1 My _____aunt_____ is a _____taxi driver_____.

2 My _____ is a _____.

3 My _____ is a _____.

4 My _____ is a _____.

1 **Listen and write.** 🎧 TR: 28

This is a farmer. His name is Zaid.

He doesn't _____ apples.

He _____ olives instead!

This is a football player. Her name is Marisol.

She _____ hit the ball.

She _____ and _____ a goal!

2 **Read and write.**

1 This farmer _____grows_____ (✓) bananas.

She ___doesn't grow___ (✗) oranges.

2 This builder _____ (✗) houses.

He _____ (✓) schools.

3 This doctor _____ (✓) people.

She _____ (✗) animals.

4 This taxi driver _____ (✗) a yellow taxi.

He _____ (✓) a black taxi.

3 **Look and write.**

1 This teacher _____ maths.

2 She _____ English.

3 This man _____ tennis.

4 He _____ football.

Reading

1 Unscramble the words. Circle the word that is the opposite of *old*.

1 krow _____

2 sue _____

3 boj _____

4 yongu _____

2 Read and write. 🎧 TR: 29

> builder   different   job   use   work   young

People all over the world play with building bricks. They are a favourite toy for boys and girls, _____ and old. But do you know, you can work with building bricks? That's right! There's a _____ called a master builder. Cool, right? Yes, but it's not easy. There are only about forty master builders in the whole world. And they _____ hard! It can take months to build a big model. Master builders _____ a lot of bricks too. One model of a German football stadium has got 1.3 million bricks!

Paul Chrzan is a master _____. Paul says, 'Just build, build, build!' He thinks it's good to build _____ things – not just what's on the box. 'Don't build the house and the spaceship,' Paul says. 'Build your family pet!'

3 Read and score from 1 (I don't agree) to 5 (I agree).

1 Being a master builder is easy.   1   2   3   4   5

2 The big models use a lot of bricks.   1   2   3   4   5

3 Building bricks are my favourite toy.   1   2   3   4   5

4 A master builder is an easy job.   1   2   3   4   5

1 Match to make sentences.

1

Does — your brother — play football for the school?
        they

Yes,   he   does.
       they   do.

2

Does   they   like baseball too?
       he

No,   he   don't.
       they   doesn't.

2 Listen and number. 🎧 TR: 30

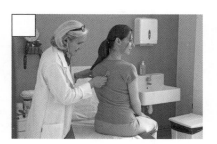

3 Write and answer questions about someone in your family.

1 Does your _____ work inside?   _____ .

2 Does _____ use a computer?   _____ .

3 Does _____ help people?   _____ .

4 Does _____ drive?   _____ .

5 Does _____ work with other people?   _____ .

1 **Listen and join the words.** 🎧 TR: 31

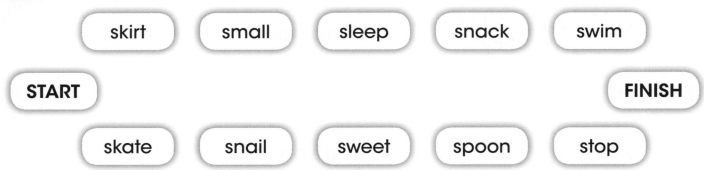

skirt   small   sleep   snack   swim

START   FINISH

skate   snail   sweet   spoon   stop

2 **Help the snail find the water. Circle the words with**
sk, sl, sm, sn, sp, st **or** *sw.* **Say.**

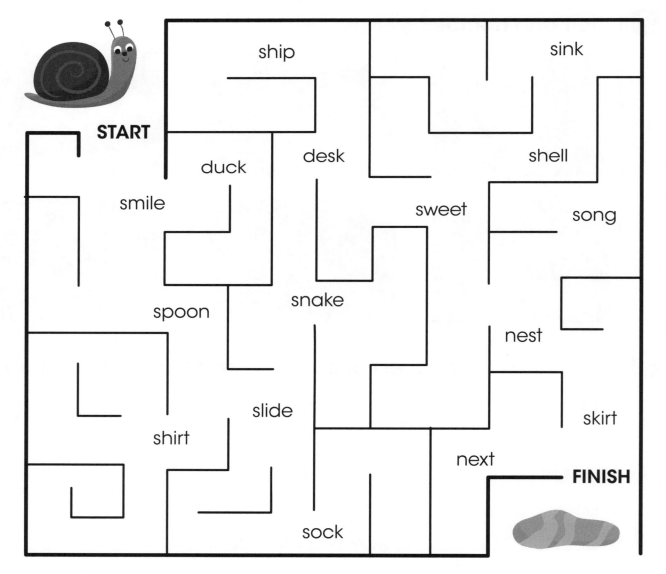

1 Read and circle the polite phrases.

Thank you. OK. No. Yes, please.

Come here. Help me now! No, thanks. Sorry, no.

2 Who is being polite? Look and tick (✓).

1

A Pass the rubber. ☐

B Pass the rubber, please. ☐

2

Would you like an apple?

A No, thanks, Dad. ☐

B No. ☐

3

Here we are.

A OK, stop here. ☐

B That's great, thank you. ☐

3 Look and write.

Would you like some cake?

1

You: _____

2

_____

1 Listen and number. 🎧 TR: 32

2 Look and write.

> do   have x 4   get x 2   go

1 _____ up

2 _____ dinner

3 _____ dressed

4 _____ homework

5 _____ breakfast

6 _____ a bath

7 _____ lunch

8 _____ to bed

I do these things in this order: _____

3 What do you do in these rooms? Write.

1 I _____ in the kitchen.

2 I _____ in the dining room.

3 I _____ in the bedroom.

4 I _____ in the bathroom.

1 **Listen and write.** 🎧 TR: 33

One o'clock, _____ o'clock, three o'clock, four.
Five o'clock, six _____, seven o'clock, more!

What's the _____? Tick-tock. It's seven o'clock.
Get up, _____ dressed. It's time for school!

What's the time? Tick-tock. It's _____.
Have dinner, have a bath. _____ for bed!

2 **Read and write the correct times. Draw the sky.**

1 It's six o'clock in the morning.

2 It's eleven o'clock in the morning.

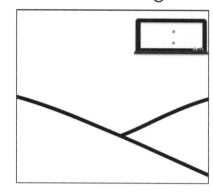

3 It's seven o'clock in the evening.

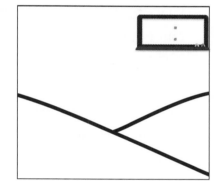

3 **Look and write.**

1

It's four o'clock in the afternoon.

2

_____

3

_____

4

_____

Reading

1 Find and circle four words from the story.

ulovechurthwaitufindo

2 Read and write. 🎧 TR: 34

> finds   hurt   love   morning   waits

This is a story about the Blooms: Mum, Dad, three boys … and a bird.

In 2013, Mum gets _____. She can't walk. One day, one of the boys _____ a baby magpie. It's hurt too. The boy brings it home. This bird is black and white, so they call her 'Penguin'. The Blooms help Penguin get better. Soon, she can fly!

Penguin helps the Blooms too. In the _____, she flies into the bedroom and the boys get up. She sits with Mum in the afternoon. At three o'clock, Penguin goes to the garden and _____. The boys come home from school. Now they can play. With Penguin, the Blooms are happy again.

One day, Penguin flies away. The Blooms _____ Penguin, but they aren't sad. Now she's with other birds!

3 Put the sentences in order.

They call the bird Penguin. ☐   One boy finds a bird.   ☐

The bird is hurt.   ☐   Penguin flies away.   ☐

Mum gets hurt.   1   Penguin helps the family. ☐

4 What do you like about this story? What don't you like?

_____

1 **Put the words in order.**

1 you / time / what / get / up / do / ?

_____

2 get / up / we / six / o'clock / at

_____

3 your / dad / time / does / what / bed / go / to / ?

_____

4 he / o'clock / eleven / at / bed / goes / to

_____

2 **Listen and write the correct times.** 🎧 TR: 35

1

2

3

4

3 **What time do you do each activity? Write.**

1 get up: I get up at _____

2 have breakfast: _____

3 do homework: _____

4 go to bed: _____

1 Listen and join the words. 🎧 TR: 36

| black | cloud | gloves | plum | flag |

START   **FINISH**

| clock | glass | floor | glue | plane |

2 Colour the picture. Say.

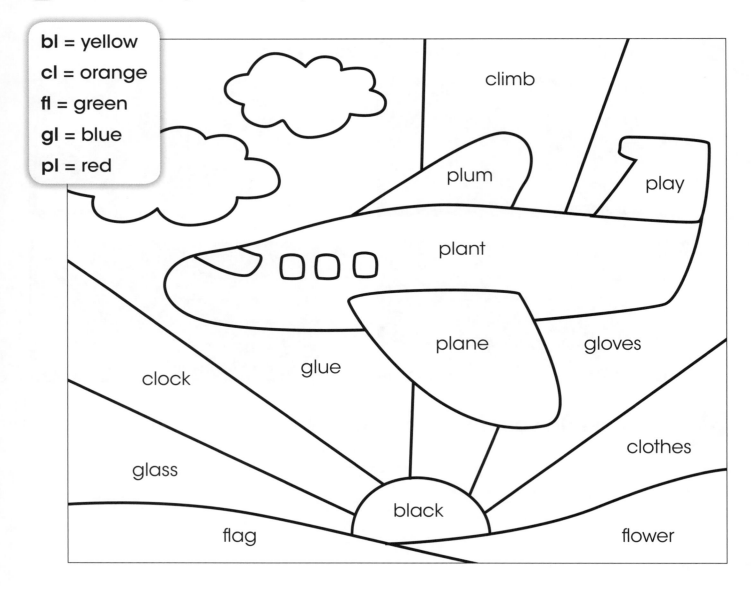

bl = yellow
cl = orange
fl = green
gl = blue
pl = red

climb
plum
play
plant
plane
gloves
glue
clock
clothes
glass
black
flag
flower

1 Who is helping others? Look and tick (✓).

1

2

3

2 Read and draw.

Look at me! I help others.

Function 2: Making and responding to suggestions

See page 132.

1 Read and circle. Listen and check. 🎧 TR: 37

Karim: Hey, Ali! **Let's / Don't** play basketball.

Ali: Sure. That **looks / sounds** fun!

Karim: Imran, do you want to play basketball too?

Imran: **Not / No** really. I want to play football. Is that OK?

Ali: **Not. / No.** I don't want to play football.

Karim: Well, we can play basketball and football!

Imran: **Good / Bad** idea!

Ali: Come on. Let's go to the **library / park**.

2 Listen and tick (✓) A or B. 🎧 TR: 38

		A	B
1	Let's go to the swimming pool.	✓	☐
2	Do you want to play hockey?	☐	☐
3	We can play football and ride our bikes.	☐	☐
4	I don't want to go for a walk.	☐	☐
5	Come on. Let's have a snack.	☐	☐
6	Do you want to watch TV at my house?	☐	☐

1 Remember the video. Circle the things that the astronauts have got.

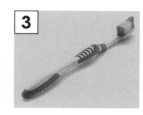

2 Read and write *T* for True or *F* for False.

1 The Earth looks green and blue from space. `F`

2 There are lots of astronauts on the ISS.

3 Everything floats in outer space.

4 Sometimes the astronauts work outside the space station.

5 The astronauts don't live on the ISS. They go home to Earth in the evening.

6 The astronauts can do exercise on the ISS.

3 Imagine you're an astronaut on the ISS. It's time to get up. Draw three things you do. (Remember that everything floats!)

1 Match.

1	do	dressed
2	score	a bath
3	drive	homework
4	have	lunch
5	go	houses
6	have	goals
7	build	to bed
8	get	a taxi

2 Find and circle eight words.

x u s e p l o v e z y o u n g h w o r k n h u r t p j o b r w a i t u f i n d q

3 Look and write.

1

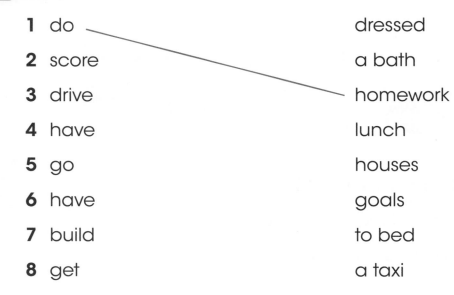

__ __ oon

2

__ __ ock

3

__ __ ag

4

de __ __

5

__ __ um

6

ne __ __

4 Read and circle.

This is Clarita. She's a taxi driver. She **gets up / get up** at seven o'clock **in / at** the morning. She doesn't **work / works** in the morning. She goes to work at one o'clock in the afternoon. She **drives / drive** her taxi around town. She doesn't **have / has** dinner at home. She **goes / go** to bed at twelve o'clock.

5 Read and answer.

1 Does Clarita go to work in the afternoon? _____

2 What time do you go to school? _____

3 Does Clarita go to bed at one o'clock in the morning? _____

4 What time do you go to bed? _____

I can ...	Yes.	I need to practise.
• talk about work and my daily routine.	☐	☐
• say what people do and don't do in their jobs.	☐	☐
• ask and answer questions with *does* about people's jobs.	☐	☐
• ask the time and say what the time is.	☐	☐
• ask and answer questions about what time I do things.	☐	☐
• read and spell words with *sk, sl, sm, sn, sp, st, sw, bl, cl, fl, gl, pl.*	☐	☐

Fantastic food

Words

1 **Match.**

1 juice
2 egg
3 beans
4 sausage
5 cheese
6 pear
7 chips
8 grapes
9 mango
10 chicken

2 **Listen and circle the food or drink that each person likes.** 🎧 TR: 39

1 mango juice / pear juice

2 chips / beans

3 cheese / eggs

4 sausages / chicken

3 **What do you like? Write six foods in order from ☹ to ☺.**

☹ _____ _____ _____

_____ _____ _____ ☺

1 **Listen and write.** 🎧 TR: 40

What have we got for breakfast today?
There's _____ bread, an egg, some orange juice too.
But _____ isn't any milk!
Oh, what can we do?

What have we got for lunch today?
_____ rice, some grapes, a mango too.
But _____ any chicken!
Oh, what can we do?

What have we got for dinner today?
_____ chips, some beans, some carrots too.
But _____ sausages!
Oh, what can we do?

2 **Read and circle.**

This is my breakfast. **There / There's** an egg. There's **a / some** bread and **there's / there are** some sausages. There **is / isn't** any juice, but there's some milk. There aren't **any / some** oranges, but there's **some / a** pear. It's a big breakfast!

3 **Look and write.**

What's for dinner?

1 There are some _____chips_____.

2 There are _____.

3 There's _____.

4 There aren't _____.

5 There _____.

Reading

1 Circle the food.

burger   get   money   put

2 Read and write. 🎧 TR: 41

burger   get   money   pizza   put   snack

You're feeling hungry and you want a _____.
You can find one at a vending machine. Just
_____ your _____ in, and there it
is! People usually buy sweets and drinks from vending
machines, but you can get much more.

What do you like for breakfast? Some vending
machines have got bread and eggs. Do you eat fruit?
You can _____ oranges or bananas too.

Is there any food for lunch and dinner in a vending machine? Yes, there
is! You can get a _____, or you can get chicken and rice. A
vending machine can even make a _____ for you!

Vending machines have got other things too: socks, jeans, books …
even cars. Imagine that!

3 Circle the things that you can't find in a vending machine.

a car   a house   a burger   a tree   a pizza   an egg

4 Draw your favourite things. Write.

In my vending machine,

_____

_____

_____

_____

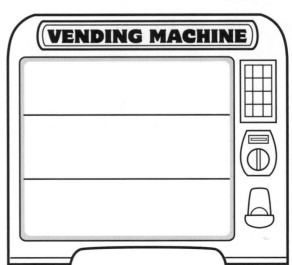

VENDING MACHINE

1 Read and write.

> a   any   are   aren't   is   isn't

1 Is there _____ milk?   Yes, there _____.

2 Is there _____ mango?   No, there _____.

3 _____ there any beans?   No, there _____.

2 Listen and write *Diego* or *Luis*. 🎧 TR: 42

1 _____   **2** _____

3 Look at the pictures in Exercise 2. Write.

Diego's lunch

1 juice   _Is there any juice_ ?   _Yes, there is._

2 pear   _____ ?   _____

3 carrots   _____ ?   _____

Luis's lunch

4 mango   _____ ?   _____

5 burger   _____ ?   _____

6 beans   _____ ?   _____

1 **Listen and circle.** 🎧 TR: 43

frog   present   great   green   draw   crab   breakfast

tree   crayon   drink   train   friend   pretty   brother

2 **Where is the treasure? Follow the path.**
Complete the words. Say.

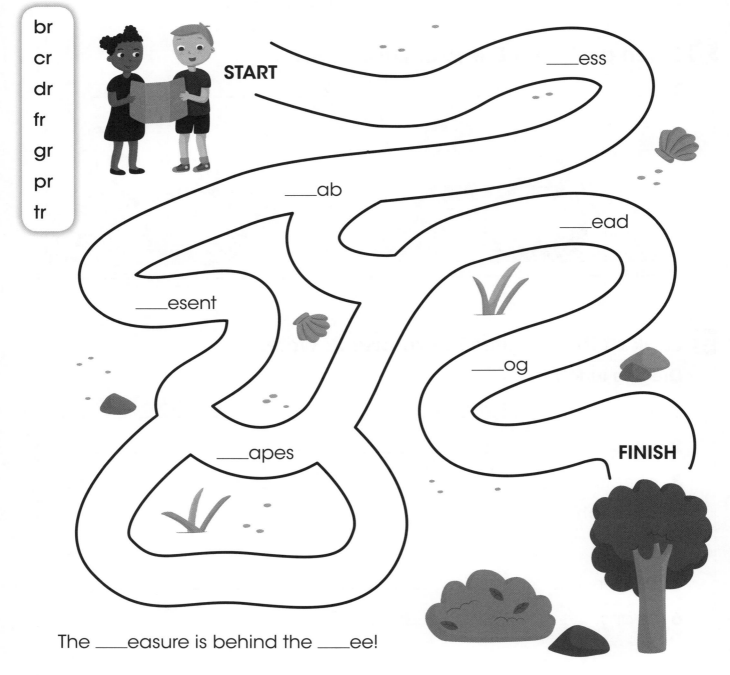

br
cr
dr
fr
gr
pr
tr

START

____ess

____ab

____ead

____esent

____og

____apes

FINISH

The ____easure is behind the ____ee!

1 Who is giving and sharing? Look and tick (✓).

1

2

3

2 Read and draw.

Look at me! I can give and share.

LESSON 1 Words

1 Listen and match. 🎧 TR: 44

1 hold — with my friends
2 take — lemonade
3 listen — an ice cream
4 dance — a balloon
5 eat — to music
6 drink — photos

A
B
C
D
E
F

2 Read and write.

> dance   drink   eat   hold   music   photos

1 Can you _____ this present for me, please?

2 Can I _____ this juice, please?

3 Can you take _____, please?

4 Can we _____ the cake now?

5 Let's _____!

6 Let's listen to _____!

3 How do you celebrate? Draw and write.

1 I _____
_____ .

2 We _____
_____ .

3 _____
_____ .

1 Listen and write. 🎧 TR: 45

It's my birthday. I'm eight today.
We're _____ a party – hooray, hooray!

_____ holding balloons and playing a game.
We're _____ cake and drinking lemonade.
My classmates are here, and _____ fun.
_____ so happy! Thank you, everyone!

It's my birthday. I'm eight today.
_____ a party – hooray, hooray!

2 Read and circle.

1 **I / I'm** eating pizza.

2 **You / You're** drinking juice.

3 **He / He's** holding a present.

4 She's **singing / sing** a song.

5 **We're / We** playing a party game.

6 They're **dance / dancing** to music.

3 Look and write.

1 She _____ photos.

2 He _____ an apple.

3 The children _____ .

4 The girls _____ .

1 **Unscramble the words. Which one can you hold? Tick (✓).**

1 valifest _____ ☐   **2** joyen _____ ☐   **3** teckub _____ ☐

2 **Read and write.** 🎧 TR: 46

| bucket   enjoying   festival   parties   street   water |

It's the Songkran _____ in
Thailand and people – young and old –
are having fun. This is the New Year for Thai
people. It usually goes on for three days.
There are lots of street _____.
People go outside and have big
_____ fights. At this festival, you
can throw water on your friends, your family
… everyone. It's fantastic!

Look at this family. They're _____ Songkran. They've got
buckets of water. This boy is holding a _____ of water. What
is he doing with that water? He's throwing it on the people in the
_____! Is that OK? Yes, of course! It's Songkran!

3 **Answer the questions about Songkran and a festival that you enjoy.**

	Songkran	**My festival**
1 How many days does it go on for?		
2 What do you do at the festival?		
3 Why do you celebrate it?		

1 Put the words in order.

1 you / are / what / doing / ?

_____

taking / I'm / photos

_____

2 your / doing / what's / brother / ?

_____

homework / he's / his / doing

_____

3 doing / they / are / what / ?

_____

dinner / having / they're

_____

4 you / what / doing / are / ?

_____

fight / having / we're / water / a

_____

2 Listen and tick (✓). 🎧 TR: 47

1 ☐  ☐

2 ☐  ☐

3 ☐  ☐

4 ☐  ☐

3 Write.

1 What _____ ? I'm _____ .

2 _____ ? My mum/dad is _____ .

3 _____ ? My classmates are _____ .

1 Listen and join the words. 🎧 TR: 48

| thing | sink | bang | long | rink |

START   **FINISH**

| think | sing | bank | link | ring |

2 Help the sheep cross the bridge. Write words with *ng* or *nk* to build the bridge. Say.

dri   lo   morni   pi   si   so   stri   ta   thi

1 Who is being grateful? Look and tick (✓).

1

2

2 Circle all the things that you are grateful for.

I've got some fun toys.

My grandparents
live near my house.

I've got a bike.

I've got homework today.

Be grateful.

I've got nice friends.

My family helps me with
my English homework.

I've got a pet.

I've got some books.

3 Read, write and draw.

This is something I'm grateful for:

_____

_____

_____

_____

1 Find and circle.

go to bed   eggs   juice   builder   taxi driver   balloon   bucket

take a photo   do homework   burger   have dinner   football player

Nasreddin and the dinner party

1 Match.

1 Nasreddin gets a letter.

2 Nasreddin isn't a rich man.

3 He puts rice on his shoes.

4 He puts fish on his shirt.

5 He puts chicken in his trousers.

A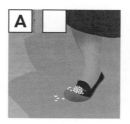

B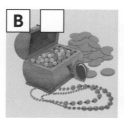

C

D

E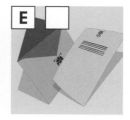

2 Underline the incorrect information. Then correct it.

1 Nasreddin is <u>playing</u> on his farm.   working

2 The rich man is having a lunch party. _____

3 At first, Nasreddin wears his party clothes. _____

4 Nasreddin feels happy at the party. _____

5 At home, Nasreddin has a shower. _____

6 Nasreddin puts the food on the floor back at the party. _____

3 Think. Score from 1 (I don't agree) to 5 (I agree). Circle.

1 Be kind to everyone, rich or poor.   1   2   3   4   5

2 Have a shower before a party.   1   2   3   4   5

3 Wear your best clothes to a party.   1   2   3   4   5

4 Enjoy the food at a party.   1   2   3   4   5

1 Circle the odd one out.

1

hold   dance   beans

2

mango   balloon   pear

3

chicken   lemonade   juice

4

listen to music   take photos   sausage

2 Find, circle and write.

r	m	o	n	e	y	f	w
e	a	t	t	b	v	s	a
o	c	h	e	e	s	e	k
f	e	s	t	i	v	a	l
i	r	n	d	r	i	n	k
u	t	e	n	j	o	y	z

1 m __ __ __y

2 e __ __

3 ch __ __ __ __

4 f __ __ __ __v __l

5 dr __ __ __

6 e __ __ __y

3 Complete the words.

br   cr   dr   fr   gr   ng   pr   tr

1 __ __ apes

2 __ __ ee

3 si __ __

4 __ __ead

5 __ __ og

6 __ __ ess

7 __ __ esent

8 __ __ ab

4 Read and circle.

1 I'm **hold / holding** a present.

2 **We're / We** listening to music.

3 There's **a / some** cheese.

4 What are you **do / doing**?

5 There **are / is** some pears.

5 Look and write.

1 Are there any balloons at the party? _____

2 What's Mum doing? _____

3 Are there any burgers on the table? _____

4 (What / Grandpa)   He's eating cake.

_____?

5 (What / children)   They're dancing.

_____?

I can ...	Yes.	I need to practise.
• name food words, and words and actions for parties.	☐	☐
• ask and talk about what food there is.	☐	☐
• talk about what people are doing.	☐	☐
• read and spell words with *br, cr, dr, fr, gr, pr, tr* and *ng*.	☐	☐

LESSON 1 Words

1 Find and circle four words. What's the secret word?

snakeltigerimonkeyocrocodilen

The secret word is _____.

2 Look and write.

1 _____

2 _____

3 _____

4 _____

3 Listen and colour the animals in Exercise 2. Write. 🎧 TR: 49

1 The _____ are brown and pink.

2 The _____ are grey.

3 The _____ are _____ and brown.

4 The _____ are _____ .

1 Listen and write. 🎧 TR: 50

Oh! There's a tiger. Is the tiger sleeping?
Shh, shh. Yes, it is.

Oh! There's a snake. Is the snake _____?
Shh, shh. Yes, it _____.

Oh! There's a crocodile. _____ the croc sleeping?
Snap, snap! No, _____!

Help! There's a crocodile. Is the croc _____?
Snap, snap! _____! SNAP!

2 Look and write.

1 you / take photos _____ Are you taking photos _____?
Yes, _____ I am _____.

2 giraffe / drink water _____?
_____.

3 lion / run _____?
_____.

4 zebras / walk _____?
_____.

3 Draw yourself in the picture. Write.

1 you / watch the monkeys
_____?
_____.

2 you / climb the tree
_____?
_____.

3 you / take photos
_____?
_____.

1 **Circle the words that are opposites. Underline the word that's an animal.**

fast   rhino   sleep   slow

2 **Read and write.** 🎧 TR: 51 | fast   friends   rhinos   sheep   sleeps |

Gertjie and Matimba are baby white _____ . They live at an animal home in South Africa. They haven't got mothers, so workers at the home are helping them.

Gertjie and Matimba have also got a friend, a _____ called Lammie. Sheep and rhinos aren't usually _____ . But Gertjie, Matimba and Lammie play together. It's fun to watch!

Lammie is small and _____ . The rhinos are bigger than Lammie, and they're slower too. Lammie is older than Gertjie and Matimba, so she looks after them. At bath time, Lammie sits next to the water. At bedtime, she _____ outside their room. They haven't got a mum, but Gertjie and Matimba are happy they've got Lammie!

3 **Write.**

1 Write two words to describe Lammie. _____small_____ _____

2 Who is older, Lammie or Gertjie? _____

3 Write two animals from the photos that aren't usually friends.

_____ _____

4 Imagine what they can do together. They can _____ and _____ together.

1 **Read and circle.**

1 A snake is **long / longer** than a monkey.

2 A mouse is a **small / smaller** animal.

3 A duck is **slow / slower** than a crocodile.

4 I'm **young / younger** than my cousin.

5 My brother is **big / bigger** and **old / older** than me.

6 My bike is **new / newer** and **fast / faster**!

2 **Listen and tick (✓) or cross (✗).** 🎧 TR: 52

1 Is a giraffe smaller than a hippo? ☐

2 Can a giraffe run faster than a hippo? ☐

3 Has a giraffe got longer legs than a hippo? ☐

4 Is a hippo slower in the water than a giraffe? ☐

5 Has a hippo got a bigger mouth than a giraffe? ☐

6 Has a hippo got a smaller head than a giraffe? ☐

3 **Write about you, your friends and your family.**

big   fast   old   short   slow   small   young

1 My friend and I: I'm _____ than my friend.

2 My _____ and I: I'm _____ .

3 _____ and _____: _____ .

1 **Listen and number.** 🎧 TR: 53

tape ☐ cape ☐ plane ☐

cap ☐ plan ☐ tap ☐

2 **Colour** *green* **the parts with** *a_e* **like in** *cake.* **Say.**
What's the hidden picture? _____

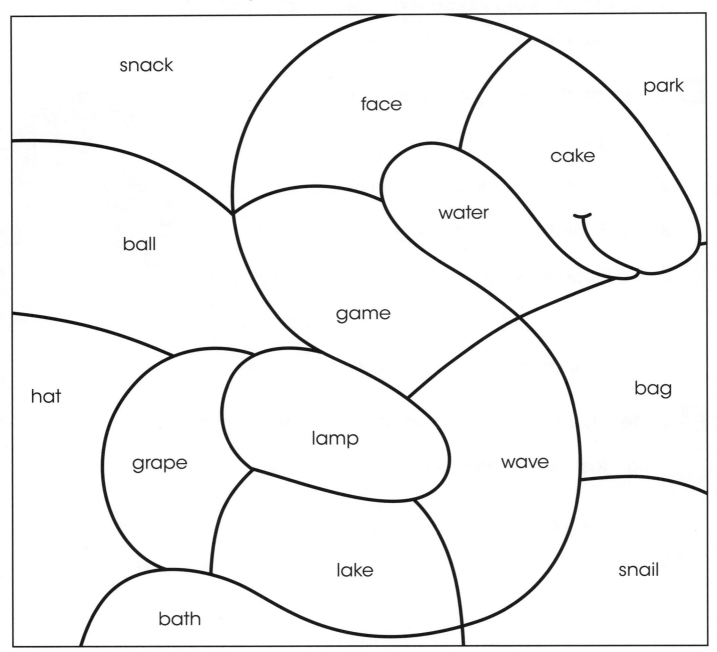

snack

face

park

cake

ball

water

game

hat

bag

grape

lamp

wave

lake

snail

bath

VALUE Be a good friend.

1 Who is being a good friend? Look and tick (✓).

Don't play football with Kenny. He's smaller and slower than us.

OK. Let's play without Kenny.

That isn't kind! Kenny's my friend. We can all play football.

2 Be a good friend. Score from 1 (OK) to 5 (very good). Circle.

1 I can share my toys.   1 2 3 4 5

2 I can help my friends.   1 2 3 4 5

3 We can play together.   1 2 3 4 5

4 I can ask 'What's the matter?'   1 2 3 4 5

3 Read and draw.

Look at me!
I can be a good friend.

1 Match.

hot

sunny

raining

cloudy

cold

windy

snowing

2 Listen and write. Draw. 🎧 TR: 54

1 _____wear_____ a mask

2 _____ some flippers

3 _____ a snorkel

4 _____put on a coat_____

5 _____

6 _____

3 What's your favourite weather? Write the weather in order from ☹ to ☺.

☹ _____ ☺

78

1 **Listen and write.** 🎧 TR: 55

Hey, hey, what's the weather like?
What's the weather _____ today?
It's cloudy. _____ raining.
I'm wearing my T-shirt.
The weather _____ today!

Hey, hey, what's the weather like?
What's _____ like today?
It's windy. _____ .
I'm wearing my coat.
_____ today!

2 **Look and write.**

What's the weather like?

1 _____It's sunny._____

2 _____

3 _____

4 _____

5 _____

6 _____

3 **What's the weather like today? Draw and write.**

_____ today.

I'm wearing _____ .

1 **Unscramble the words. Circle the words for things you see outside.**

1 kys _____

2 gorfet _____

3 waibron _____

4 ghribt _____

2 **Read and write.** 🎧 TR: 56 | brighter   forget   rainbow   sky   violet |

What is a rainbow?

It's a colourful arc in the _____. A rainbow has got red, orange, yellow, green, blue and _____. But rainbows haven't always got six colours. Morning rainbows are red, orange and yellow – you can't see the other colours.

What weather makes a rainbow?

Rain and sun make a rainbow. Bigger raindrops make _____ rainbows. To find a rainbow, stand with the sun behind you. Don't _____ your umbrella! Now, look up.

Can I make a rainbow?

Yes, you can. Bring a glass of water and some white paper to a sunny window. Hold the glass above the paper. Sunlight goes through the water and makes a _____ on the paper.

3 **Colour and write. Don't forget the order of the colours.**

1 a morning rainbow

It's got these colours:

_____

2 an afternoon rainbow

It's got these colours:

_____

1 Look and circle.

1

Wear / Don't wear your boots inside.

2

It's cold. **Put on / Don't put on** your gloves.

3

It's raining. **Forget / Don't forget** your umbrella today.

4

It's snowing. **Wear / Don't wear** your scarf today.

2 Listen. Write *T* for True or *F* for False. 🎧 TR: 57

1 It's raining today.   ☐

2 Freddie tells Jakob to wear a T-shirt.   ☐

3 Freddie says they can play games on Jakob's tablet.   ☐

4 Freddie asks Jakob to bring his swimming trunks.   ☐

5 They can ride their bikes to the park.   ☐

3 Read and write suggestions.

1 It's snowing today.

_____ Put on a coat. _____

_____

Don't _____ .

2 It's sunny today.

_____

_____

Don't _____ .

1 **Listen and circle.** 🎧 TR: 58

1 time / Tim   2 like / lick   3 lime / lit

4 kite / kit   5 bite / bit   6 bike / bin

2 **Help the bird find the nest. Circle the words with *i_e* like in *kite*. Say.**

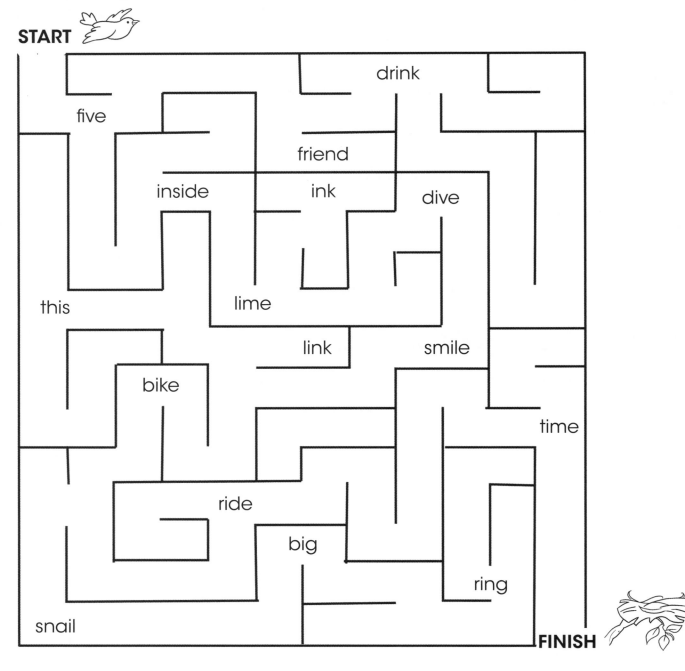

START

five
drink
friend
inside   ink   dive
this   lime
link   smile
bike
time
ride
big
ring
snail
FINISH

1 ## Who is looking after themselves? Look and tick (✓).

1 Which boy is looking after himself?

2 Which girl is looking after herself?

2 ## The weather is hot today. How do you look after yourself? Tick (✓).

1 Put on gloves. ☐

2 Put on a coat. ☐

3 Don't wear a sun hat. ☐

4 Don't forget your sun hat. ☐

5 Drink lots of water. ☐

6 Forget your water bottle. ☐

7 Bring your water bottle. ☐

8 Wear a T-shirt. ☐

3 ## Read, circle and draw.

This is how I look after myself in **hot / cold / windy** weather:

Function 3: Being polite

See page 132.

1 **Read and circle. Listen and check.** 🎧 TR: 59

Oliver:	**Help / Excuse** me. Please can I see those orange football boots?
Shop assistant:	Sure. Here you are.
Oliver:	Oh, they're too small. Can I **like / have** some bigger ones?
Shop assistant:	I'm **sorry / happy**. I haven't got any bigger ones in orange.
Oliver:	That's OK. Oh, I love those basketball shoes. Can I see them?
Shop assistant:	**Sure / Sorry**. Here you are. They look great on you!
Oliver:	Yes, **I'd like / I want** these shoes. How much are they?
Shop assistant:	They're 25 euros.
Oliver:	Here you **are / do** – 25 euros.
Shop assistant:	Thank you! Have a nice day!

2 **Write the phrases below in a polite way.**

> Excuse   Here you are   I'd like   Please can you   sorry

1 Hey! ⟶ _____ me.

2 Give me that apple! ⟶ _____ give me that apple?

3 Here. Take it. ⟶ Sure. _____.

4 I want some juice. ⟶ _____ some juice, please.

5 No. ⟶ I'm _____.

1 Remember the video. Tick (✓) the things that go in Tian Tian's cake.

bamboo ☐   bananas ☐   beans ☐

carrots ☐   pears ☐   water ☐

2 Look, read and write.

1 What is the zookeeper making?   a _____

2 How old is Tian Tian today?   _____

3 What shape is Tian Tian's cake?   a _____

4 Where is Tian Tian?   _____

5 What is Tian Tian doing?   He's _____ his cake.

3 Write.

1 What do you eat at a party?

_____

_____

2 How do people in your country celebrate when they are sixteen?

_____

_____

1 Circle the odd one out.

1 rainbow   giraffe   raining

2 coat   elephant   hippo

3 sunny   monkey   rhino

4 snowing   cold   hot

5 cloudy   zebra   windy

6 lion   crocodile   tiger

2 Circle six words. Find the secret word.

s l e e p s f o r g e t c s k y a f a s t r b r i g h t f s l o w

The secret word is _____.

3 Look and write.

Words with *a_e*	Words with *i_e*
cake	

4 Look and write.

1 Is it snowing?

_____

2 What's the weather like?

_____

3 Is the tiger sleeping?

_____

4 Is the elephant bigger than
the monkey?

_____

5 Look at the picture in Exercise 4. An explorer is going to this place. Make some suggestions.

1 (forget)
<u>Don't forget
your hat.</u>

2 (bring)

_____

_____

3 (forget)

_____

_____

4 (wear)

_____

_____

I can ...	Yes.	I need to practise.
• talk about animals and the weather.	☐	☐
• ask and answer about what animals are doing.	☐	☐
• compare animals.	☐	☐
• ask and answer questions about the weather.	☐	☐
• make suggestions about clothes for the weather.	☐	☐
• read and spell words with _a_e_ and _i_e_.	☐	☐

LESSON 1 Words

1 Listen and number. 🎧 TR: 60

☐ bus ☐ car ☐ helicopter ☐ lorry

☐ motorbike ☐ plane ☐ ship

2 Write.

It goes on water.	
It goes on land.	car
It goes in the sky.	

3 Write about getting to school and coming home.

1 I go to school by _____. **2** I come home by _____.

3 I get to school at _____. **4** I get home at _____.

1 Listen and write. 🎧 TR: 61

_____ do you _____ school?
By bus or car or train?
I go to school by bus. Then it brings me home again.

_____ does your school bus _____?
At six or seven or eight?
It comes at seven o'clock, but now and then it's late!

_____ your school bus _____
after you get to school?
It goes past the library, the shops, the playground and the pool.

2 Put the words in order. Match.

1 school / do / how / to / you / get / ?

_____

2 to / do / when / you / get / school / ?

_____

3 do / have / lunch / you / where / ?

_____

4 do / when / you / get / home / ?

_____

I have lunch at school. ☐

I get home at five o'clock. ☐

I go by bike. ☐

I get to school at nine o'clock. ☐

3 Write three questions to ask a friend.

| do homework   get home   get to school   go   have lunch |

1 How _____?

2 Where _____?

3 When _____?

1 Find and (circle) four words from the reading. <u>Underline</u> the word that has got days in it.

p h e a l t h y i m o n t h i r e a d y u s n a c k y

2 Read and write. 🎧 TR: 62 | healthy   lorry   months   ready   snack

Bananas are a _____ _____ . But they grow in hot, sunny countries. I'm from Poland – that's far! So, how does this banana get into my hand?

1 Bananas start as flowers on a banana plant. After about nine _____ , the farmer takes the bunch off the plant. They're still green.

2 Workers look at the bananas. If the bananas look OK, the workers put them into boxes. These boxes of bananas go by _____ to a shipyard.

3 Now the bananas are ready for a long trip. They go by ship to Europe. It can take around fourteen days.

4 In Europe, lorries bring the bananas to towns and cities. There, shop workers put the bananas out. Now I can get some and bring them home. When they're yellow, they're _____ to eat!

3 How do the bananas get from the farm to people's homes?

1 The bananas go by **motorbike / lorry** from the farm to the shipyard.

2 The bananas go by **ship / plane** to other countries.

3 The bananas go by **lorry / train** to the shop.

4 Write.

1 Choose a fruit: _____ Does it grow in your country? _____

2 How does it get to your home? _____

1 Listen and write. 🎧 TR: 63

It's Saturday morning. There are _____ on the roads. There are _____ in the streets. The market is busy. The fruit stall has got _____ of fruit. People are buying _____ and hats. People are eating different _____ of food. _____ are playing in the park. It's busy on Saturday.

2 Write.

	One	Two or more		One	Two or more
1	tooth	_____	4	mouse	_____
2	woman	_____	5	beach	_____
3	foot	_____	6	fish	_____

3 Write about your home and family.

1 in my house / baby   In my house, there aren't any babies.

2 in my family / child   _____

3 in our kitchen / mango   _____

4 in our fridge / tomato   _____

5 in our garden / sheep   _____

Phonics

1 **Listen and number.** 🎧 TR: 64

hop ☐   cone ☐   hot ☐   note ☐   not ☐   hope ☐

2 **Help the driver. Write words with *o_e* to fill up the car with fuel. Say.**

b dr h n r thr

ome one ope ose ote

throne

VALUE Know your food.

1 Who knows where their food comes from?
Look and tick (✓) or cross (✗).

2 Match.

 1

 A

 2

 3

 B

 4

 C

 D

 5

 E

3 Read and draw.

I know where my food comes from.

1 Match.

 1
 2

clean
kind
clever
quiet
silly
dirty
naughty
loud

 3
 4

 5
 6

 7
 8

2 Listen and match. 🎧 TR: 65

Anna

Dan

Jill

Tom

Nick

3 Draw and write about you and your friend.

This is me.
I'm _____
_____ .

This is my friend.
_____
_____ .

1 **Listen and write.** 🎧 TR: 66

Growing up, growing up!

I _____ loud at three years old.

_____ naughty at four years old.

I was _____ at five years old.

Growing up, growing up!

_____ quiet at six years old.

_____ at seven years old.

Now I'm eight, _____ as good as gold!

2 **Read and circle.**

1 When I was little, I **was** / **'m** silly. Now, I **was** / **'m** quiet.

2 Before, my sister **was** / **is** naughty all the time. Now, she **was** / **'s** good.

3 This story **was** / **is** scary when I **was** / **is** young.

4 Now I **was** / **'m** eight, this story **wasn't** / **isn't** scary.

5 After football, my brother **was** / **is** really dirty. Now, he **wasn't** / **isn't** dirty. He **was** / **'s** clean.

6 When I **was** / **is** little, my mum **was** / **wasn't** a doctor. Now, she **was** / **is**!

3 **Write about you and someone in your family.**

	✓	✗
I	tiny	
My _____		

When I was little, _____ .

When my _____ was little, _____ .

1 **Circle the word that is the opposite of** *child*. **Underline the word that means** *drawing*.

cartoon   famous   funny   grown-up

2 **Read and write.** 🎧 TR: 67

cartoons   famous   fantastic   funny   grown-up   talent

Charles was a quiet boy. He wasn't good at schoolwork or sport. Some of his classmates weren't very kind to him. But Charles was good at art. His pictures were very _____ .
They were _____!

Look at the photo. Do you know this dog? It's Snoopy. Charles is Charles Schulz, the creator of Snoopy and the *Peanuts* _____ . Today, people around the world love this silly, black–and–white dog, his owner Charlie Brown and their friends, the Peanuts Gang.

As a child, Charles Schulz's life wasn't easy. As a _____ , Charles Schulz was a _____ artist. Art was his _____ . What's your talent?

3 **Write and draw.**

1 What's the name of Schulz's famous cartoon?

_____ .

2 What's Snoopy like?
He's _____ .

3 Who's your favourite cartoon character?
It's _____ .

4 What's he/she like?

_____ .

Draw your favourite cartoon character.

1 Sam is talking to his grandma. Match the sentences.

1 What was I like as a baby?

They were silly.

But you were loud!

2 What were Dad and Uncle Jim like?

You were good.

But we were happy.

3 What were you and Grandpa like?

We weren't rich.

But they weren't naughty.

2 Listen and write. Tick (✓). 🎧 TR: 68

Our dad _____ happy with us today. We _____ on a family trip to the zoo. The animals _____ interesting, but my sisters _____ loud and silly. Then we _____ even quiet at lunchtime. Our dad was angry. It _____ a good day!

A

B

3 Write.

What were you and your friends like in class today?

_____

Phonics

1 **Listen and circle.** 🎧 TR: 69

1 huge / hug   2 cute / cut   3 tube / tub

4 use / us   5 cube / cub

2 **Colour *yellow* the words with *a_e*. Colour *red* the words with *i_e*. Colour *orange* the words with *o_e*. Colour *green* the words with *u_e*. Say.**

1 **What talents have the children got? Look and write.**

1

Sasha

This maths isn't easy.

Really? I love it!

What is Sasha's talent?

_____

2

Ezana

You're so good!

Thanks. I love it.

What is Ezana's talent?

_____

2 **Who has got these talents? Write the name of a friend, someone in your family or a famous person.**

1

_____

2

_____

3

_____

4

_____

5

_____

6

_____

3 **What's your talent? Write and draw.**

My talent is:

_____

_____

_____

Game 3

1 Do the wordsearch. Write.

q	u	i	e	t	o	l	b	a	s
m	z	p	d	l	s	h	i	p	c
h	e	l	i	c	o	p	t	e	r
z	e	b	r	a	g	u	d	a	o
s	h	r	t	l	o	r	r	y	c
p	s	o	y	b	r	h	i	n	o
r	a	i	n	b	o	w	m	h	d
y	n	e	g	w	i	n	d	y	i
s	n	o	w	i	n	g	k	j	l
b	n	a	u	g	h	t	y	d	e

1

zebra

2

3

4

5

6

7

8

9

10

11

12

Cars: then and now

1 **Listen and write.** 🎧 TR: 70

> 1880s   1910s   1950s   Today

1
Cars are colourful.

2
Cars are cleaner and quieter.

3
A black car with one window is popular.

4
Cars are slow, but faster than a horse.

2 **Read and write *T* for True or *F* for False.**

1 Karl Benz's car was faster than a bicycle. ☐

2 The Ford Model T was a colourful car. ☐

3 The Ford Model T was good to drive when it was windy. ☐

4 Cars in the 1950s weren't bigger than cars in the 1910s. ☐

5 Cars today are smaller and quieter than in the 1950s. ☐

6 Robots can drive some cars. ☐

3 **Read and score from 1 (I don't agree) to 5 (I agree).**

When I grow up, …

1 I'd like a pink car.   1 2 3 4 5

2 I'd like an electric car.   1 2 3 4 5

3 I'd like a robot to drive my car.   1 2 3 4 5

4 I'd like a bike, not a car.   1 2 3 4 5

1 Unscramble the words.

1 y c a r s

_ _ _ _ _ _

2 t o m o r k e b i

_ _ _ _ _ _ _ _ _ _

3 t i l t e l

_ _ _ _ _ _

4 n e l a p

_ _ _ _ _

5 n a c l e

_ _ _ _ _

6 r y r l o

_ _ _ _ _

2 Read and write the words in the correct column.

~~bus~~ car famous funny kind plane ship silly

Words for transport	Words to talk about people
bus	

3 Look and write in the correct column.

Words with *o_e*	Words with *u_e*
home	

4 **Listen and write a word or a number.** 🎧 TR: 71

1 What number bus stops here?
Number _____5_____

2 When does the bus come?
_____ o'clock

3 Where does the bus go?   to _____ Street

4 What was the little boy like this morning?   He was _____.

5 What time does art class start?   _____ o'clock

6 How does the girl get home?   by _____

5 **Write. Use was/were (✓), wasn't/weren't (✗) and the correct form of the word in brackets.**

1 The school _____buses_____ (bus) _____were_____ (✓) late this afternoon.

2 When I _____ (✓) little, I _____ (✗) quiet.

3 In class today, some _____ (child) _____ (✓) naughty.

4 There _____ (✓) some colourful _____ (scarf) in that shop.

I can ...	Yes.	I need to practise.
• talk about how to get to school or work, and describe people and things.	☐	☐
• ask and answer questions about getting around.	☐	☐
• write words for two or more things: *babies, tomatoes, dishes.*	☐	☐
• talk about when I was little with *was* and *wasn't.*	☐	☐
• talk about what other people were like with *were* and *weren't.*	☐	☐
• read and spell words with *o_e* and *u_e.*	☐	☐

1 **Remember the video. Circle the types of transport that you saw.**

1

2

3

4

2 **Read and write.** dangerous famous raining ride slow walls

This is the _____ Yungas Road in Bolivia. This road is very _____. Cars and lorries on this road are very _____. There aren't any _____ on the side of the road. Also, the weather changes all the time. It's sunny, then it's cloudy and then it's _____! Some people _____ their bikes on this road. That's scary!

3 **Imagine you're on the Yungas Road. How are you getting to the next town? Draw and write.**

bike car lorry motorbike skateboard unicycle beautiful
cool dangerous fantastic fun horrible long quiet scary

I'm going by

_____.

The Yungas Road is

_____.

It's also _____.

The best present of all

1 Listen. Read and tick (✓). 🎧 TR: 72

1 ☐ In this story, the old woman is kind. She gives a jewel to a young man. At first, the young man wants to buy a big house and new clothes. At the end of the story, he doesn't want those things. He wants to be kind.

2 ☐ In this story, the old woman is kind. She gives a jewel to a young man. The young man buys a big house and new clothes. He wants to be rich. The old woman sees him again and now he's happy.

2 Underline the incorrect information in each sentence. Write the correct word.

1 An old woman stops at a stream to <u>eat some food</u>. <u>drink some water</u>

2 She finds a beautiful, green jewel in the water. _____

3 She meets a young man and he doesn't like the jewel. _____

4 The old woman says he can borrow the jewel. _____

5 In the town, the young man looks at the small houses. _____

6 The young man wants to be rich like the old lady. _____

3 Think. Score from 1 (I don't agree) to 5 (I agree).

1 The best present is the jewel.   1 2 3 4 5

2 The best present is being kind.   1 2 3 4 5

3 It is important to be rich.   1 2 3 4 5

4 It is important to be kind.   1 2 3 4 5

Listen and draw lines. There is one example. 🎧 TR: 73

Tim   Matt   Ben   Eva

Hugo   Grace   Alex

Read the question. Listen and write a name or a number. There are two examples. 🎧 TR: 74

Examples

What class is this?	2C
What is the new classmate's name?	Alice

Questions

1 How old is Alice? _____

2 What is the name of Alice's cat? _____

3 Where does Alice live? in _____ Street

4 What's her bus number? _____

5 How old is her brother? _____

Listen and tick (✓) the box. There is one example. 🎧 TR: 75

What is between the trees?

A ✓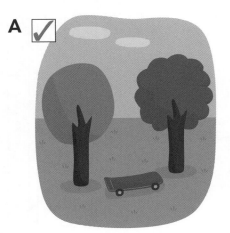

B ☐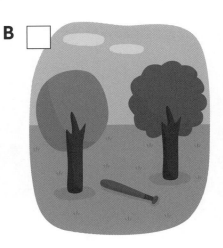

C ☐

1 What lessons has Lucy got on Tuesday?

A ☐

B ☐

C ☐

2 What time does Sam get up on Saturday?

A ☐

B ☐

C ☐

3 What is in Grandma's fridge?

A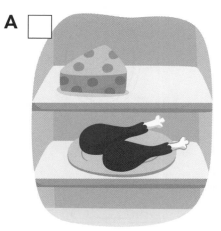

B

C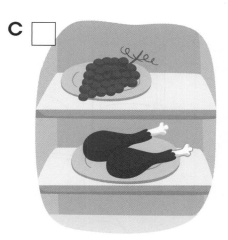

4 Where is Tom's tablet?

A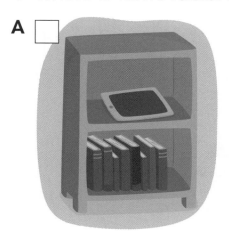

B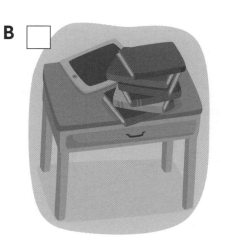

C

5 What does Jill's dad do?

A

B

C

Listen and colour. There is one example. 🎧 TR: 76

**Look and read. Put a tick (✓) or a cross (✗) in the box.
There are two examples.**

Examples

 This is our car. ✗

 This is a balcony. ✓

Questions

1  This is a camera. ☐

2  These are mangoes. ☐

3  This is grape juice. ☐

4  This is a rhino. ☐

5 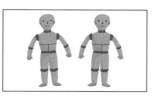 These are robots. ☐

Look and read. Write yes or no.

Examples

There are six chairs in the dining room.	yes
It's raining outside.	no

Questions

1	The lamp is between the window and the door.	_____
2	The family is eating burgers and chips.	_____
3	The boy is smaller than his sister.	_____
4	There is some bread on the table.	_____
5	It's three o'clock in the afternoon.	_____

Look at the pictures. Look at the letters. Write the words.

Example

c a r

Questions

1

_ _ _ _

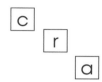

2

_ _ _ _ _

3

_ _ _ _ _

4

_ _ _ _ _ _ _ _ _ _

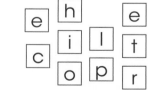

5

_ _ _ _ _ _ _ _

Read this. Choose a word from the box. Write the correct word next to numbers 1–5. There is one example.

Elephants

African ___elephants___ are bigger than Asian elephants. How do you know if you are looking at an Asian or an African elephant? Look at their ears. Asian elephants have got smaller (1) _____ .

Elephants eat (2) _____, grass and fruit. They love (3) _____! Elephants haven't got a (4) _____, they've got a trunk. They use their trunks for drinking, eating, holding things, smelling things and squirting water.

Can elephants swim? Yes, they can! They use their trunks like a (5) _____. That's very clever!

Example

elephants

bananas

snorkel

hippo

eyes

ears

nose

plants

Look at the pictures and read the questions.
Write one-word answers.

Examples

What's the weather like?   sunny

What's the dad holding?   two ____raincoats____

Questions

1 What's the girl putting on?   a _____

2 What are the children doing?   playing _____

3 How do they feel?   _____

4 What is the weather like now?   It's _____ .

5 What have the children got?   an _____

Look at the picture. Read the questions and point.

Where is the teacher?

Where is the box of fruit?

Where is the tablet?

Read and draw.

Where is the bus? Put the bus behind the tree.

Where is the football? Put the football between the boy and the girl.

Where are the grapes? Put the grapes next to the bananas.

Where is the baseball bat? Put the baseball bat in front of the box of fruit.

Look at the picture. Answer the questions.

1 Where is this class?

2 Have these students got PE on Tuesday?

3 What fruit is there in the box?

4 Find the clock. What's the time?

5 Look at the sky. What's the weather like?

6 Tell me about the teacher and the students. What are they doing?

Look at the pictures. Answer the questions.

1  2  3  4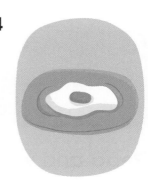

Questions

1 What's this?
Have you got a bike?
How do you get to school in the morning?

2 What's this?
What day have you got music?
What's your favourite lesson?

3 What's this?
Are you loud or quiet?
Were you silly when you were younger?

4 What's this?
Do you have eggs for breakfast?
What's your favourite food?

Starters Speaking **Part 4**

Answer the questions.

How old are you?

Where do you live?

What have you got in your house?

Lesson 2   Preposition *on* + day of the week

Use **on** + Monday, Tuesday, etc. to say when something happens.							
on	Monday	Tuesday	Wednesday	Thursday	Friday	Saturday	Sunday
I've got English **on** Monday.							

Read and write *on* and the correct day of the week.

1 I've got music ___on Thursday___ .

2 I've got science _____ .

3 I've got English _____ .

4 I've got PE _____ .

Monday	English
Tuesday	maths
Wednesday	PE
Thursday	music
Friday	science

Lesson 4   *have got*

I	**'ve got**	maths on Monday.
He She	**'s got**	
Note: 've got = have got 's got = has got		

Have	I	got maths on Monday?	Yes, I	**have**.
			No, I	**haven't**.
Has	he she		Yes, he she	**has**.
			No, he she	**hasn't**.
Note: haven't = have not hasn't = has not				

Read and circle.

1 He (**'s got**)/ **'ve got** English on Thursday.

2 I **'s got** / **'ve got** PE on Tuesday.

3 **Have** / **Has** you got art on Monday? Yes, I **have** / **has**.

4 Has he **have** / **got** music on Tuesday? **Yes** / **No**, he hasn't.

5 **Have** / **Has** Maria got reading on Friday? Yes, she **have** / **has**.

Lesson 2   Demonstrative adjectives: *this, these, that, those*

This is her skateboard.
This isn't his skateboard.

That's her bike.
That isn't his bike.

These are his building bricks.
These aren't her building bricks.

Those are his felt-tip pens.
Those aren't her felt-tip pens.

Note:
that's = that is
isn't = is not
aren't = are not

Read and write.

1   _____ **This isn't** _____ (✗)
his robot.

2   _____ (✗)
my felt-tip pens.

3   _____ (✓)
your camera.

4   _____ (✓)
your pencils.

Lesson 4   Possessive *'s*

Add **'s** to a person's name to say that an object belongs to him or her.
This is Milo**'s** tablet. Anna**'s** skateboard is yellow.

Look and write.

Spiro

1   _____ This is Spiro's tablet. _____

2   _____

Mei

Calla

3   _____

4   _____

Sam

Lesson 2 *We/They've got; our, their*

We've got a big table.	
They've got a small table.	
I've got	She's got
You've got	We've got
He's got	They've got

Possessive adjectives	
This is **our** table. That's **their** table.	
my	her
your	our
his	their

Read and circle.

1 This is **our / their** living room. We've got a rug on the floor.

2 These are their books on the bookshelf. **We've / They've** got a lot of books.

3 **Our / Their** balcony is cool! They've got a fantastic house!

4 Our garden is big. **We've / They've** got trees and flowers in the garden.

Lesson 4 Prepositions *in front of, behind, between*

 The ball is **in front of** the bag.

 The ball is **behind** the bag.

 The ball is **between** the bags.

Look and write. Use *in front of, behind* or *between*.

1 The armchair is
   between the bookcase and the window .

2 The lamp is _____ .

3 The cat is _____ .

4 The window is _____ .

Lesson 2 Present simple with *I, you, we, they*

I You We They	play	football. tennis.	**Note:** don't = do not
	don't play		

Put the words in order.

1 goals / they / football / in / score

_____

2 tennis / play / with / my / sister / I

_____

3 bounce / ball / you / the / in / basketball

_____

4 play / we / hockey / the / don't / in / park

_____

Lesson 4 Present simple questions and answers with *I, you, we* and *they*

Do	I you we they	play football?	Yes,	I you	do.
			No,	we they	don't.

Write.

1 Do you catch the ball in basketball? _____

2 Do we kick the ball in tennis? _____

3 (hit / ball / baseball) _____ Yes, you do.

4 (throw / ball / hockey) _____ No, they don't.

Lesson 2 Present simple with *he* and *she*

This farmer He She	grow**s**	apples.
	doesn't grow	
My cousin He She	teach**es**	science.
	doesn't teach	

Note: With *he/she* add *s* to the verb: *I grow* but *he grows*. *We help* but *she helps*. For the verbs *catch, teach* and *watch,* add *es*: *Mum teaches art*.

Read and write. (build grow help teach)

1 This doctor ____helps____ (✓) animals. She _____ (✗) people.

2 This teacher _____ (✓) art. She _____ (✗) maths.

3 This builder _____ (✗) schools. He _____ (✓) houses.

4 This farmer _____ (✓) rice. He _____ (✗) potatoes.

Lesson 4 Present simple questions and answers with *he* and *she*

| **Does** | he
she | **work** outside? | Yes, | he
she | **does**. |
| | | | No, | he
she | **doesn't**. |

Read and write.

1 _____ she help people?   Yes, she does.

2 Does he work inside?   No, he _____ .

3 Does your mum _____ (use) a computer? Yes, she does.

4 _____ your dad drive to work?   Yes, he _____ .

Lesson 2 Telling the time

What's the time?	Note: Write times as a number: *It's **7:00*** or as a word: *It's **seven o'clock***. When you want to say the time of day, add *in the morning, in the afternoon* or *in the evening*. *It's three o'clock **in the afternoon***.
It's seven o'clock/7:00.	
It's eight o'clock/8:00.	

Look and write.

1 What's the time? (2:00) _____

2 What's the time? (5:00) _____

3 _____? It's three o'clock.

4 What's the time? It's eleven o'clock _____.

Lesson 4 *What time do/does ... ?, at + time*

What time	do	I/you we/they	have lunch?	I/You We/They	have lunch	at twelve o'clock. at one o'clock.
	does	he/she		He/She	has lunch	

Read and circle.

1 What time **do / does** you get up? I get up **in / at** 7:00.

2 What time **do / does** you get to school? We get to school **at 9:00 / 9:00**.

3 What time **do / does** your sister have lunch? She has lunch **at / to** 1:00.

4 What time **do / does** the children go to bed? They go to bed **at / in** 7:00.

Lesson 2 *There is/are; some* and *any*

There's	a an	pear. apple.	**Note:** There's = There is
	some	cheese.	isn't = is not
There **are**	three some	eggs.	aren't = are not egg**s**, apple**s**, grape**s** =
There **isn't**	any	juice. grapes.	there **are** some there **aren't** any
There **aren't**			cheese, juice, milk = there **is** some there **isn't** any

Read and write.

1 There / orange / lunch tray (✓)   There's an orange on my lunch tray.

2 There / tomatoes / table (✓)   _____

3 There / grapes / lunchbox (✗)   _____

4 There / grape juice / table (✓)   _____

Lesson 4 *Is there/Are there ... ?; some* and *any*

Is there	any	milk	in the fridge?	Yes,	there is.
				No,	there isn't.
Are there		chips	on the table?	Yes,	there are.
				No,	there aren't.

Read and write.

1 Is there any cheese in the fridge?   (✓) _____

2 Are there any burgers in the fridge?   (✗) _____

3 _____ juice in the fridge?   (✗) _____

4 _____ eggs in the fridge?   (✓) _____

Lesson 2   Present continuous affirmative (*be* + verb + *-ing*)

I'm You're He's She's We're They're	hold**ing** a balloon. tak**ing** photos.	I'm = I am You're = You are He's = He is She's = She is We're = We are They're = They are	**Note:** hold + ing → holding take + ing → taking

Read and circle.

1 I'm **eat / eating** a burger.

2 **We / We're** listening to music.

3 He's **take / taking** photos.

4 You're **hold / holding** a present.

5 She's **dancing / dance**.

6 **They / They're** playing a game.

Lesson 4   Present continuous questions (with *what*)

What	am are 's are	I you he she we they	doing?	I'm You're He's She's We're They're	throw**ing** water.
Note: What's = What is					

Read and write.

1 What are you doing?

(drink) We _____ lemonade.

2 What _____ I doing?

You're eating cake.

3 What _____ he doing?

(take) _____ photos.

4 What _____ they doing?

(dance) _____

Lesson 2 Present continuous questions and answers

Am	I			I	am.		I	'm not.
Are	you			you	are.		you	aren't.
Is	he she it	go**ing**?	Yes,	he she it	is.	No,	he she it	isn't.
Are	we they			we they	are.		we they	aren't.

Note: run + n + ing → running, sit + t + ing → sitting

Read and write.

1 Am I _____ (play)?   Yes, you _____.

2 _____ you sleeping?   No, we _____.

3 Is he _____ (eat)?   Yes, _____.

4 _____ taking photos?   Yes, I _____.

Lesson 4 Comparative adjectives: *-er than*

Use comparative adjectives to compare one thing with another thing.			
I'm	fast**er**	**than**	my brother.
An elephant is	big**ger**		a rhino.

Note: big + g + er → bigger

Read and write.

1 Lions are fast. Cows are slow. → Lions are (fast) _____.

2 A giraffe is big. A mouse is small. → A giraffe is (big) _____.

3 This crocodile is small. That crocodile is big. → (small) _____

4 You're eight. Your brother is twelve. → (young) _____

Lesson 2 *What's the weather like? It's + weather*

What's the weather **like**?	**It's** cold. / **It's** hot.
	It's cloud**y**. / **It's** sun**ny**. / **It's** wind**y**.
	It's rain**ing**. / **It's** snow**ing**.
Note: cloud + y → cloudy, sun + n + y → sunny, rain + ing → raining	

Look and write. Draw the weather in number 4.

 **1** What's the weather like?
_____

 **2** What's the weather like?
_____

 3 What's the weather like?
_____

4 _____?
It's raining.

Lesson 4   Imperatives

| Use the imperative form to tell a person to do something. **Wear** your coat. **Put on** your boots. | **Note:** Don't = Do not |
| Use *Don't* + verb to tell a person **not** to do something. **Don't wear** your scarf. **Don't bring** an umbrella. | |

Read and write. Use *Don't* if necessary.

1 It's raining. _____ (forget) your umbrella.

2 It's windy today. _____ (put on) your scarf.

3 You haven't got English today. _____ (bring) your English book.

4 It's sunny today. _____ (wear) your sun hat.

Lesson 2   Questions with *How ...?*, *When ...?*, *Where ...?*

How	do you get to school?	I go by bus.
When	does the bus come?	It comes at eight o'clock.
Where	does he have lunch?	He has lunch at school.

Read and circle. Match.

1 How **do / does** they get to school?

2 When does the bus **come / comes**?

3 **When / Where** do you have lunch?

4 **How / Where** does your mum get to work?

A We have lunch at school.

B She goes by bus.

C They go by bike.

D It comes at eight o'clock.

Lesson 4   Irregular plurals

	one	two or more
+ es	beach	beaches
	box	boxes
	bus	buses
	dress	dresses
	fox	foxes
	mango	mangoes
	potato	potatoes
	tomato	tomatoes
no change	fish	fish
	sheep	sheep

	one	two or more
y → ies	baby	babies
	family	families
	party	parties
f → ves	scarf	scarves
other	child	children
	foot	feet
	man	men
	mouse	mice
	person	people
	woman	women

1  tomatoes

2 _____

3 _____

4 _____

5 _____

6 _____

Lesson 2   Past simple: *was, wasn't*

I He She It	**was**	good at school.
	wasn't	

Note: wasn't = was not

Read and circle.

1 Before, his face **is / was** dirty. Now, it **'s / was** clean.

2 When I **'m / was** little, I was loud. Now, I **'m / was** quiet.

3 The book **isn't / wasn't** scary, it was funny!

4 When my dad **is / was** little, he **'s / was** silly and funny!

5 Before, I **'m not / wasn't** big. Now, I **'m / was** big.

Lesson 4   Past simple: *were, weren't*

You We They	**were**	famous.
	weren't	

Note: weren't = were not

Read and write.

1 My friends _____ (✓) naughty at school today.

2 We _____ (✗) silly at the park today.

3 You _____ (✓) cute when you were a baby.

4 We _____ (✗) very kind when we were younger.

5 They _____ (✗) quiet at the library this afternoon.

Functions

Function 1: Talking about feelings

How are you feeling today?	I'm feeling happy/tired/sad/angry/hungry/thirsty.
Are you OK?	I'm fine, thanks.
What's the matter?	Nothing's the matter!

Function 2: Making and responding to suggestions

Do you want to play basketball?	Sure. That sounds fun! Not really.
Let's go to the playground.	Good idea!

Function 3: Being polite

Excuse me.	Sure. Here you are.
Please can I see/have ...?	I'm sorry. I haven't got ...
I'd like ...	That's OK.

Unit 1

art
bath
birthday
class
computers
English
garden
homework
lesson
maths
music
PE
reading
science
Thursday

Unit 2

bike
borrow
brother
building bricks
camera
cool
felt-tip pens
guitar
new
old
robot
skateboard
tablet
these
this

Unit 3

armchair
balcony
bookcase
chair
dining room
door
fish
floor
inside
lunch
mirror
outside
rug
shop
stairs
wall
window

Unit 4

baseball
basketball
bounce
catch
different
duck
easy
fantastic
hit
hockey
jump
kick
pink
sink
socks
team
tennis
throw

Wordlist

Unit 5	Unit 6	Unit 7	Unit 8
build	black	beans	angry
builder	clock	bread	balloon
doctor	do homework	burger	bucket
drive	find	cheese	dance
farmer	flag	chicken	drink
football player	get dressed	chips	eat
grow	get up	crab	enjoy
help	glass	dress	festival
job	go to bed	egg	hold
score goals	have a bath	frog	lemonade
skirt	have breakfast	get	listen to music
slide	have dinner	grapes	long
small	have lunch	juice	sing
snack	hurt	mango	take photos
spoon	love	money	
stop	plum	pear	
swim	wait	present	
taxi driver		put	
use		sausage	
work		tree	
young			

Unit 9

cake

crocodile

elephant

fast

game

giraffe

hippo

lion

monkey

rhino

sleep

slow

snake

tiger

zebra

Unit 10

bike

bright

bring an umbrella

cloudy

cold

forget

hot

kite

put on a scarf

rainbow

raining

sky

snowing

sunny

time

wear a coat

windy

Unit 11

bus

car

come home

cone

get to school

healthy

helicopter

home

lorry

month

motorbike

nose

plane

ready

ride a bike

ship

snack

Unit 12

cartoon

clean

clever

cube

cute

dirty

famous

funny

grown-up

kind

little

loud

naughty

quiet

scary

silly

tube